Trouble
on the Trail

Linda M. Washington
Illustrated by Tony Caldwell

Rigby®

A Harcourt Achieve Imprint

www.Rigby.com
1-800-531-5015

Literacy by Design Leveled Readers: *Trouble on the Trail*

ISBN-13: 978-1-4189-3666-2
ISBN-10:   1-4189-3666-9

Printed in China
3 4 5 6 7 8 985 14 13 12 11 10 09 08

Contents

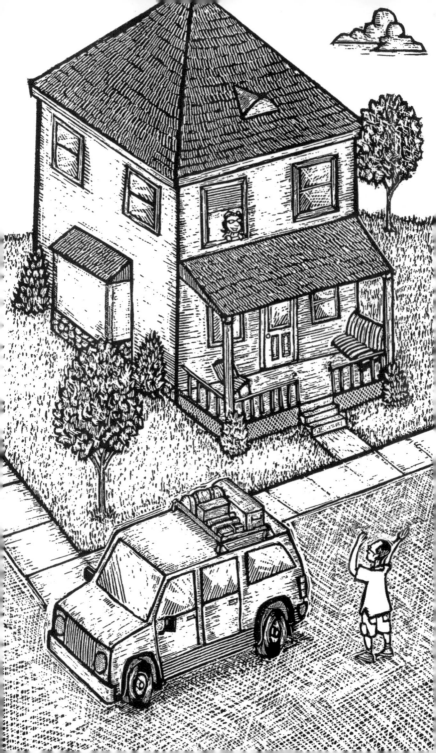

Chapter 1

Hurry Up, Carmen!

"Hurry up, Carmen!" her father yelled from outside.

Carmen could tell from the tone of his voice that *Papá* was anxious to leave, so she leaned out her bedroom window and answered, "OK, *Papá*!"

As she ran out the back door, she thought of her canteen. She had just filled it with water, but where was it now? A quick look in her backpack sent her back inside the house.

"I hope you have everything now," Carmen's younger brother Alex said when she climbed into the back seat of the car.

"Carmen, you are so forgetful!" *Mamá* said. "Did you remember to put the first-aid kit in your backpack like I asked?"

"Yes, *Mamá*," said Carmen, poking Alex, "but I thought you had the first-aid kit. You're the nurse."

Papá started the car and cheered, "Big Bend National Park, here we come!"

Carmen couldn't wait to get to the park and practice what she had learned in her camping and hiking classes. "I just hope I can remember everything I learned," she thought.

Chapter 2

The Warning

The trip to Big Bend took several hours, but Carmen's first glimpse of the magnificent Chisos Mountains made the long drive worth it. When she got out of the car, she stood and stared in wonder at the huge green and gray rocks rising up on the horizon.

When they went inside the visitor's center to get a map and permits for hiking, Alex grumbled, "I didn't know we'd need permission to walk around."

The woman at the center smiled and told them, "The park can be dangerous if you don't know what you're doing. Therefore, you'll need to be careful during your visit. Also, a mountain lion was seen near the campsite, so please try to avoid hiking at night. If you see a mountain lion, leave it alone. However, if it looks like it is going to attack, wave your arms and throw stones."

Carmen's heart skipped a beat. Would they see a mountain lion near the camp? She tried to remember what she had been taught about mountain lions.

As she helped her father pitch the tent that evening at the campsite, she looked around the area. Could there be a mountain lion nearby?

Suddenly she heard *Mamá* scream! Carmen spun around, catching a glimpse of a small, black scorpion crawling out of *Mamá's* rolled-up sleeping bag. "Don't move!" Carmen warned *Mamá*.

Mamá froze until the scorpion scurried away, and then she said, "That scorpion startled me!"

"In class the teacher told us to always shake out our shoes and check under rocks for scorpions," Carmen said. "I was so busy thinking about mountain lions that I forgot to tell you."

"I'll remember that next time," *Mamá* promised, eyeing her sleeping bag uncertainly.

Chapter 3

Danger on the Trail

The next day, as Carmen and her family set out to hike some trails surrounding the Chisos Mountains, *Papá* reminded them to stay together and make their water last.

Alex asked hopefully, "Do you think we'll see a mountain lion today?"

"Probably not, because we'll be back before nightfall, and that's when they wander around the land," *Papá* answered.

"This will be an easy hike," Alex said, sounding disappointed.

"Hiking five miles is not so easy, and this park is full of mountains, deserts, scorpions, and wild animals," *Mamá* told him.

Papá led the way down a canyon trail lined with oak and pine trees, and they passed a field of bluebonnets that were lifting their blue and white faces to the sun. But before the family went very far, Carmen had to return quickly to the campsite to grab her forgotten canteen.

13

Farther along the trail, Carmen spotted a tiny bird, its wings a blur, in a field of wildflowers and called out, "Look at that hummingbird!"

Alex said, "I'd rather hike a harder trail so that we can see a bigger animal like a bear or even a deer!"

"We'll go on a harder trail next time, but I want a problem-free day today," *Papá* said.

As the trail wound up a steep hill and through a desert of rocks and prickly pear cacti, Alex suddenly darted ahead, shouting, "I'll race you to the top!"

Papá reached for Alex, calling, "Alex, be careful or you might fall over the edge!"

"*Papá*, the stones are loose!" Carmen yelled, watching in horror as *Papá* slipped on a stone and fell down the edge of the hill!

Chapter 4

A Big Problem

Carmen and Alex stared down in breathless fear as *Papá* lay on the ground at the bottom of the hill. Then *Papá* groaned, and they sighed in relief.

Carmen held Alex back from rushing down the hill, saying, "We need to go slowly so we don't fall, too." When they reached the bottom of the hill, *Papá* was just starting to sit up.

Mamá asked him gently, "Are you hurt at all?"

"I'm . . . a little shaken, but I think I can get up," *Papá* said.

But when he stood up and tried to walk, he cried out in pain, "My ankle—something's wrong with it!"

"Let me see it," *Mamá* said, and *Papá* leaned against a rock while she gently looked at his ankle.

"It's beginning to swell, and I think it's broken," *Mamá* concluded in a worried voice. "You won't be able to walk very far on it, so we're going to need to get help from the rangers at the station."

"*Papá,* I want to stay with you because it's my fault that you're hurt," Alex said softly.

"And I'll go with you, *Mamá,* because I know lots of things about hiking safely," offered Carmen.

"Just be careful," *Papá* said.

"We will, and I'll leave my canteen with you so you'll have plenty of water," *Mamá* said.

Carmen quickly checked the supplies in her backpack: canteen, flashlight, water bottle, marking tape, granola bars, knife, whistle, map, compass. "I hope that's all we'll need," she thought with concern.

Carmen suddenly felt afraid. The sun was low and red on the horizon, and it would be getting dark soon.

Chapter 5

Carmen's Quest

Before they left, Carmen and *Mamá* checked the map, and *Mamá* pointed to the right, saying, "The rangers' station is about five miles that way."

Following *Mamá* down the trail, Carmen paused after a few steps and looked back at *Papá* one last time. He smiled bravely and waved, and she felt her heart race with determination to find help for him as quickly as possible.

A short way down the trail, Carmen wrapped some marking tape around the branch of a tree, where it was easily visible. "We'll use this tape to help us find our way back to *Papá*," she thought to herself. She marked another farther down the trail, wondering if *Mamá* could see her doing this through the darkness of the night. Of course, *Mamá* seemed too concerned about *Papá* to notice much of anything.

21

After a while, the trail led them through a forest of oak trees where the rough branches waved and danced in the soft evening wind. The breeze and the noise of the rustling leaves made Carmen feel a little better.

The next part of the trail climbed steadily through prickly shrub that had been easier to see in the daytime. As they hiked up the trail, Carmen's legs felt scratched all over.

"Why don't we try to find a different trail without these prickly bushes?" *Mamá* suggested.

"We shouldn't take shortcuts because we might get lost," Carmen warned *Mamá*.

Just as they neared the top of a hill, Carmen heard something moving in a group of shrubs to the right of the trail. "What's that?" she hissed, aiming her flashlight beam in that direction.

Chapter 6

Danger in the Dark

With a sudden rustle of grass, a jackrabbit leaped out of the brush, pausing for a moment before glancing at Carmen and her mother and hopping away.

"Whew, I thought it was a javelina," Carmen gasped, weak with relief that a fat javelina wasn't charging at them with its razor-sharp tusks.

"It's the snakes that worry me, not the javelinas," *Mamá* said grimly, examining the shadows under the brush.

"Let's take a water break," said Carmen, checking a nearby large rock for scorpions before settling down on it. "I know my canteen is in my backpack somewhere."

"I'm thirsty, too, but I gave your father my canteen," *Mamá* said with regret.

"I brought an extra water bottle," Carmen told *Mamá,* reaching into her backpack for it.

"Good girl," *Mamá* praised Carmen, accepting the water bottle gratefully.

"Let's see how much farther we have to go now," *Mamá* suggested, handing the map to Carmen. Carmen had *Mamá* point the flashlight's beam onto the map while Carmen placed her compass against it, just as she had been taught to do in class.

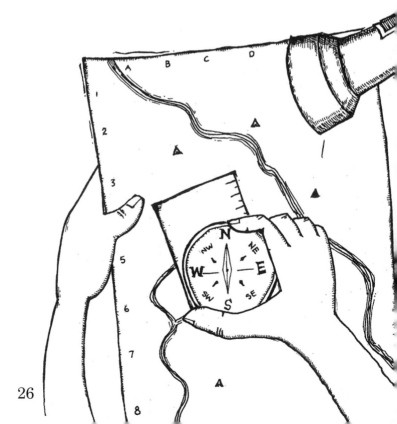

"We need to go north two more miles—that way," Carmen said, pointing to the left.

Suddenly the mournful cry of a coyote could be heard from that direction, followed seconds later by the low growl of a different animal.

"Do you think that was a mountain lion?" Carmen asked, feeling goose bumps spring up along her arms. "It sounded like one I heard on TV once."

"I hope not, but we'd better get going just in case," *Mamá* said.

But just as Carmen turned to go, something flew at her face from a nearby tree!

Chapter 7

Hunted!

"**B**rrrrut—brrrut—brrrrut!" the creature's croaks sounded like rumbling explosions inside of a tin can. Carmen yelped in surprise and stumbled backward over a rock, landing on the ground. Still trembling, she told her heart to slow its wild beating—the animal was only a tree frog.

Just as she was feeling better and sitting back to dust the dirt off of her hands, she heard a soft rattling nearby. Slowly a snake slid out of the shrub next to her.

"Carmen, move this way quickly," *Mamá* hissed, her voice trembling with worry.

But Carmen slid slowly away, keeping her eyes on the snake the whole time. Once she was a safe distance from the snake, she sank against a tree, her knees shaking.

"Carmen, that was a poisonous rattlesnake! Why didn't you move when I told you to?" *Mamá* scolded.

29

"My hiking class teacher told me that rattlesnakes strike if they're surprised, so I didn't want to move too fast," Carmen explained.

Mamá hugged her and said, "That's my girl! I'm glad we're almost at the rangers' station. Let's hope nothing else happens!"

Carmen was pleased that the moon was full tonight because it made it easier for them to see where they were going. Still, the silvery moonlight created strange shadows in the grasses and trees around them, and Carmen nervously peered around for animals before taking each step. She tried to move softly—like a panther she had once read about—but the crackling branches and twigs under her feet made her sound like an elephant. Minutes later Carmen heard the low growl again. It seemed closer, and her heart pounded in fear.

"I hope we get to the rangers' station soon," Carmen said quietly to *Mamá*.

"There's no place for us to hide from animals around here," *Mamá* murmured back, waving a hand at the small shrubs, cacti, and stones around them.

"When we get to the top of that hill, we should be able to see the rangers' station," Carmen said hopefully. Suddenly a terrible smell blew under her nose, and a herd of javelinas burst out of the shrub several yards ahead of her and crossed the trail heading west.

Waving her hand in front of her nose, Carmen wondered what had caused the javelinas to run. But she didn't have long to wonder because seconds later she saw an animal slowly move into view at the top of the hill: a mountain lion.

Chapter 8

Trail's End

For a few moments, Carmen could only stand there, frozen in terror, staring at the dark shape of the mountain lion under the pale moonlight. Then the mountain lion took a step toward them, and *Mamá* took a step back, pushing Carmen behind her. As the lion moved toward them, Carmen suddenly remembered something the woman at the visitor's center had said. Immediately Carmen began waving her arms and throwing stones toward the mountain lion.

The mountain lion paused, then turned away with a snarl.

Just as Carmen sank to the ground in relief, the sound of running feet could be heard coming down the trail toward her and *Mamá*. "I think the rock-throwing noises came from over there," a man's voice called out. Two men in rangers' uniforms soon appeared with flashlights, and one asked, "Are you two OK?"

Carmen and *Mamá* quickly told the rangers that *Papá* had hurt himself and stayed behind on the trail with Alex while they went for help.

"We can drive out to help your husband if you can lead us back to him," one of the rangers explained to *Mamá*.

"Oh, I didn't think about getting back!" *Mamá* cried out. "How will we ever find where they are?"

"I marked the trees and bushes along the path with yellow marking tape," Carmen said, patting her backpack of supplies.

"That was good thinking!" one of the rangers praised Carmen. "Now it will be much easier to find your father and brother."

And sure enough, as they drove to the place where *Papá* and Alex waited, the yellow tape could be easily seen marking different points along the trail.

37

Papá and Alex were very glad to see them. When *Mamá* told *Papá* all that Carmen had done, *Papá* hugged Carmen and said, "I'm so proud of you."

"The nearest hospital is over 100 miles away, so we'll take you back to your camp first so you can pack up your belongings," one of the rangers said.

"I'm just sorry that we have to end our trip so quickly," *Papá* commented sadly.

"I think we've had enough adventures for one trip, *Papá*," Carmen laughed.

At the hospital, while a doctor looked at *Papá's* ankle, the rangers said good-bye and told Carmen, "Because you were so brave, we would like to make you a junior ranger." One of the rangers handed Carmen a badge that she pinned proudly onto her shirt.

As Carmen picked up her backpack, she suddenly noticed that her canteen was missing. She smiled shyly and asked, "Has anyone seen my canteen?"